The Ultim
Slow C(
Cookbook

Energize Your Body, Boost Metabolism and
Lose Weight Fast with Quick and Easy
Recipes.
Burn Fat and Get Lean without Feeling
Hungry.

Melissa Upton

Additionally, the information in the following pages is intended only for informational purposes and should thus be thought of as universal. As befitting its nature, it is presented without assurance regarding its prolonged validity or interim quality. Trademarks that are mentioned are done without written consent and can in no way be considered an endorsement from the trademark holder.

Table of Contents

.... 2

TABLE OF CONTENTS.. 5

INTRODUCTION 7

CRAZY CAULIFLOWER AND ZUCCHINI SURPRISE.................. 10

QUINOA AND VEGGIES 12

SPAGHETTI SQUASH BOWLS.. 14

AMAZING CURRY 16

LENTILS AND LEMON SOUP... 18

AUTUMN VEGGIE MIX... 20

SPECIAL VEGGIE STEW.. 22

VEGAN CHICKPEAS WINTER MIX 24

INDIAN LENTILS MIX 26

"BAKED" BEANS 28

SQUASH CHILI 30

RICH LENTILS SOUP 32

EASY LENTILS MIX 34

QUINOA AND BEANS CHILI 36

POTATOES AND SPINACH MIX.. 38

RICH WHITE BEAN SOUP 40

INTENSE TOFU AND PINEAPPLE MIX 42

VEGAN JAMBALAYA... 44

PORK CHOPS 46

SPICY PORK & SPINACH STEW 48

STUFFED TACO PEPPERS... 51

LAMB BARBACOA.. 54

PORK CHILE VERDE 57

HAM SOUP... 60

MINCED PORK ZUCCHINI LASAGNA... 63

BEEF DIJON.. 66

CABBAGE & CORNED BEEF.. 69

CHIPOTLE BARBACOA... 72

CORNED BEEF CABBAGE ROLLS... 75

CUBE STEAK 79

RAGU 81

ROPE VIEJA 84

SPINACH SOUP 86

MASHED CAULIFLOWER WITH HERBS.. 88

KALE QUICHE... 90

SPINACH STUFFED PORTOBELLO 92

POACHED SALMON 94

COD AND VEGETABLES 96
BALSAMIC BEEF POT ROAST 98
MOIST AND SPICY PULLED CHICKEN BREAST 101
WHOLE ROASTED CHICKEN 102
POT ROAST BEEF BRISKET 104
SERIOUSLY DELICIOUS LAMB ROAST 106
LAMB PROVENÇAL 108
GREEK STYLE LAMB SHANKS 110
HOMEMADE MEATBALLS AND SPAGHETTI SQUASH 112
BEEF AND CABBAGE ROAST 114
SIMPLE CHICKEN CHILI 116
BEEF SHOULDER IN BBQ SAUCE 117
DRESSED PORK LEG ROAST 119

Introduction

Slow cookers can be really useful in the kitchen and can make life so much easier. They make it so that you can prep your ingredients the day before, and they will be ready for you when you get home. The slow cooker is also great for people on a tight budget, because it can save you a lot of money in the long run. That said, it's important to know how to use your slow cooker properly. Here are some tips to help you get started.

Cook With Low Heat

Always start with low heat when cooking your ingredients in a slow cooker. If you put them over medium heat, they will burn or scorch before they are finished. Instead, start out on low heat and let them cook for several hours until they are done. This will ensure that they are safe to eat and don't have any nasty flavors left over from being cooked too fast.

Leave room at the top

Place your ingredients in the cooker as soon as possible after placing them on the stove top or in the oven. This will give them enough time to cook properly without being overcooked on high heat. If you leave them sitting in the hot pot without food inside of it, sometimes it can become stuck and won't release until you turn off the burner. This can cause some parts of your dish to be overcooked, which can ruin everything you worked so hard to perfect!

Use recipes right away

A great way to use your slow cooker is by developing some new recipes! Have fun experimenting and working on some new ones all at once without having to worry about any nasty flavors ruining your dish later on. Take note of what works well and what does not, so you end up with something delicious every time!

Slow Cookers are a great way to prepare your food and make it taste like someone else has done it for you. With the right recipe in your slow cooker, you can turn days of cooking into hours of preparation.

We've decided to share with you some of our favorite slow cooker recipes from around the country. Some recipes are classic favorites, while others are new and fresh. Whatever you're looking for, you'll find it here.

Slow cookers are a great way to prepare all kinds of meals. With the right recipe, you can cook a variety of dishes, including soups that will warm you up on a cold day.

Some of the advantages to using a slow cooker include reducing the amount of energy needed to use your electric stove. You also don't have to worry about burning yourself when using the stove. You can also leave the slow cooker on when you're not home, making it easy to prepare simple meals and snacks for your family.

You can find many recipes in our slow cooker cookbook. It's divided into several sections, including breakfast, main dishes, side dishes, desserts, and drinks. The slow cooker cookbook is designed for a number of different uses. For example, you can use it to make lots of different side dishes and desserts while you're on vacation or traveling. You can also use the same cookbook in your kitchen to prepare healthy main meals during the week or when you're having friends over for dinner.

Don't let your slow cooker get rusty with age! Contact us today to order our slow cooker cookbook at our guaranteed lowest price. We'll even ship it right away so that you can get started cooking immediately!

Crazy Cauliflower and Zucchini Surprise

Preparation time: 10 minutes
Cooking time: 3 hours and 30 minutes
Servings: 4
Ingredients:

- 1 cauliflower head, florets separated

- 2 garlic cloves, minced

- ¾ cup red onion, chopped

- 1 teaspoon basil, dried

- 2 teaspoons oregano flakes

- 28 ounces canned tomatoes, chopped

- ¼ teaspoon red pepper flakes

- ½ cup veggie stock

- 5 zucchinis, cut with a spiralizer

- A pinch of salt

- Black pepper to the taste

Directions:

1. Put cauliflower florets in your slow cooker.

2. Add garlic, onion, basil, oregano, tomatoes, stock, pepper flakes, salt and pepper, stir, cover and cook on High for 3 hours and 30 minutes.

3. Mash cauliflower mix a bit using a potato masher.

4. Divide zucchini noodles in bowls, top each with cauliflower mix and serve.

5. Enjoy!

Nutrition:

Calories: 302g,

Fat: 22g,

Carbs: 5g,

Protein: 34g,

Quinoa and Veggies

Preparation time: 10 minutes
Cooking time: 4 hours
Servings: 4
Ingredients:

- 1 tablespoon olive oil

- 1 and ½ cups quinoa

- 3 cups veggie stock

- 1 yellow onion, chopped

- 1 carrot, chopped

- 1 sweet red pepper, chopped

- 1 cup green beans, chopped

- 2 garlic cloves, minced

- 1 teaspoon cilantro, chopped

- A pinch of salt

- Black pepper to the taste

Directions:

1. Put the stock in your slow cooker.

2. Add oil, quinoa, onion, carrot, sweet pepper, beans, cloves, salt and pepper, stir, cover and cook on Low for 4 hours.

3. Add cilantro, stir again, divide on plates and serve.

4. Enjoy!

Nutrition:

Calories: 302g,

Fat: 22g,

Carbs: 5g,

Protein: 34g,

Spaghetti Squash Bowls

Preparation time: 10 minutes
Cooking time: 8 hours
Servings: 4
Ingredients:

- 5 pounds spaghetti squash, peeled

- 2 cups water

- 2 cups broccoli florets, steamed

- 1 tablespoon sesame seeds

- Chopped peanuts for serving

- ½ batch salad dressing

- For the salad dressing:

- 1 tablespoon palm sugar

- 1 tablespoon ginger, grated

- 3 tablespoons rice wine vinegar

- 3 tablespoons olive oil

- 2 tablespoons peanut butter

- 1 tablespoon soy sauce

- 3 garlic cloves, minced

- 1 teaspoon sesame oil

- ½ teaspoon sesame seeds

Directions:

1. In your blender, mix ginger with sugar, vinegar, oil, soy sauce, garlic, peanut butter, sesame oil and ½ teaspoon sesame seeds, pulse really well and leave aside.

2. Put the squash in your slow cooker, add the water, cover and cook on Low for 8 hours.

3. Leave squash to cool down, cut in halves, scrape flesh and transfer into a bowl.

4. Add broccoli florets, 1 tablespoon sesame seeds, chopped peanuts and the salad dressing.

5. Toss salad well and serve.

6. Enjoy!

Nutrition:

Calories: 102g,

Fat: 22g,

Carbs: 5g,

Protein: 34g,

Amazing Curry

Preparation time: 10 minutes
Cooking time: 4 hours
Servings: 6
Ingredients:

- 3 cups sweet potatoes, cubed

- 2 cups broccoli florets

- 1 cup water

- 1 cup white onion, chopped

- 28 ounces canned tomatoes, chopped

- 15 ounces canned chickpeas, drained

- ¼ cup quinoa

- 29 ounces canned coconut milk

- 1 tablespoon garlic, minced

- 1 tablespoon ginger root, grated

- 1 tablespoon turmeric, ground

- 2 teaspoons vegan tamari sauce

- 1 teaspoon chili flakes

Directions:
1. Put the water in your slow cooker.

2. Add potatoes, broccoli, onion, tomatoes, chickpeas, quinoa, garlic, ginger, turmeric, chili flakes, tamari sauce and coconut milk.

3. Stir, cover and cook on High for 4 hours.

4. Stir your curry again, divide into bowls and serve.

5. Enjoy!

Nutrition:

Calories: 302g,

Fat: 22g,

Carbs: 5g,

Protein: 34g,

Lentils and Lemon Soup

Preparation time: 10 minutes

Cooking time: 6 hours

Servings: 6

Ingredients:

- 1 yellow bell pepper, chopped

- 1 yellow onion, chopped

- 6 carrots, chopped

- 4 garlic cloves, minced

- A pinch of cayenne pepper

- 4 cups veggie stock

- 3 cups red lentils, dried

- 3 cups water

- A pinch of sea salt

- 1 tablespoon rosemary, chopped

- Zest and juice from 1 lemon

Directions:

1. Put the stock and water in your slow cooker.

2. Add bell pepper, onion, carrots, garlic, lentils, cayenne and salt.

3. Stir, cover and cook on Low for 6 hours.

4. Add rosemary, lemon zest and juice, stir, ladle into bowls and serve.

5. Enjoy!

Nutrition:

Calories: 332g,
Fat: 22g,
Carbs: 5g,
Protein: 34g,

Autumn Veggie Mix

Preparation time: 10 minutes
Cooking time: 4 hours and 30 minutes
Servings: 6
Ingredients:

- 2 sweet potatoes, cubed

- 1 yellow onion, chopped

- 1 small cauliflower head, florets separated

- 14 ounces canned coconut milk

- 2 teaspoons Sirach sauce

- 3 tablespoons coconut aminos

- A pinch of salt

- 1 tablespoon palm sugar

- 3 tablespoons red curry paste

- 1 cup green peas

- 8 ounces white mushrooms, roughly chopped

- ½ cup cashews, toasted and chopped

- ¼ cup cilantro, chopped

- A few basil leaves, chopped for serving

- Brown rice for serving

Directions:

1. Put coconut milk in your slow cooker.

2. Add potatoes, onion, cauliflower florets, sriracha sauce, aminos, salt, curry paste and sugar, stir, cover and cook on Low for 4 hours.

3. Add mushrooms, peas, cilantro and basil, stir, cover and cook on Low for 30 minutes more.

4. Divide into bowls and serve with brown rice on the side and toasted cashews on top.

5. Enjoy!

Nutrition:
Calories 376,
Fat 18.5,
Fiber 3,
Carbs 29.43,
Protein 23

Special Veggie Stew

Preparation time: 10 minutes
Cooking time: 4 hours
Servings: 8
Ingredients:

- 1 yellow onion, chopped

- 1 teaspoon olive oil

- 2 red potatoes, chopped

- A pinch of salt and black pepper

- 1 tablespoon stevia

- 1 tablespoon curry powder

- 1 tablespoon ginger, grated

- 3 garlic cloves, minced

- 30 ounces canned chickpeas, drained

- 1 green bell pepper, chopped

- 2 cups veggie stock

- 1 red bell pepper, chopped

- 1 cauliflower head, florets separated

- 28 ounces canned tomatoes, chopped

- 1 cup coconut milk

- 10 ounces baby spinach

Directions:

1. In your slow cooker, mix oil with onion, potatoes, salt, pepper, stevia, curry powder, ginger, garlic, chickpeas, red and green bell pepper, stock, cauliflower, tomatoes, spinach and milk, stir, cover and cook on High for 4 minutes.

2. Stir your stew again, divide into bowls and serve.

3. Enjoy!

Nutrition:

Calories 176,

Fat 18.5,

Fiber 3,

Carbs 29.43,

Protein 23

Vegan Chickpeas Winter Mix

Preparation time: 10 minutes

Cooking time: 4 hours and 10 minutes

Servings: 6

Ingredients:

- 1 yellow onion, chopped

- 1 tablespoon ginger, grated

- 1 tablespoon olive oil

- 4 garlic cloves, minced

- A pinch of salt and black pepper

- 2 red Thai chilies, chopped

- ½ teaspoon turmeric powder

- 2 tablespoons gram masala

- 4 ounces tomato paste

- 2 cups veggie stock

- 6 ounces canned chickpeas, drained

- 2 tablespoons cilantro, chopped

Directions:

1. Heat up a pan with the oil over medium high heat, add ginger and onions, stir and cook for 4-5 minutes.

2. Add garlic, salt, pepper, Thai chilies, garam masala and turmeric, stir, cook for 2 minutes more and transfer everything to your slow cooker.

3. Add stock, chickpeas and tomato paste, stir, cover and cook on Low for 4 hours.

4. Add cilantro, stir, divide into bowls and serve.

5. Enjoy!

Nutrition:

Calories 176,
Fat 18.5,
Fiber 3,
Carbs 29.43,
Protein 23

Indian Lentils Mix

Preparation time: 10 minutes
Cooking time: 8 hours
Servings: 16
Ingredients:

- 4 garlic cloves, minced

- 4 cups brown lentils

- 2 yellow onions, chopped

- 1 tablespoon ginger, grated

- 4 tablespoons olive oil

- 1 tablespoon garam masala

- 4 tablespoons red curry paste

- 2 teaspoons stevia

- 1 and ½ teaspoons turmeric powder

- A pinch of salt and black pepper

- 45 ounces canned tomato puree

- ½ cup coconut milk

- 1 tablespoon cilantro, chopped

Directions:

1. In your slow cooker, mix lentils with onions, garlic, ginger, oil, curry paste, garam masala, turmeric, salt, pepper and stevia.

---

2. Also add tomato puree, stir, cover and cook on Low for 7 hour and 20 minutes.

3. Add coconut milk and cilantro, stir, cover and cook on Low for 40 minutes.

4. Divide into bowls and serve.

5. Enjoy!

Nutrition:

Calories 376,

Fat 18.5,

Fiber 3,

Carbs 29.43,

Protein 23

"Baked" Beans

Preparation time: 10 minutes
Cooking time: 12 hours
Servings: 6
Ingredients:

- 1 pound navy beans, soaked overnight and drained

- 1 cup maple syrup

- 1 cup vegan BBQ sauce

- 4 tablespoons stevia

- 1 cup water

- ¼ cup tomato paste

- ¼ cup mustard

- ¼ cup olive oil

- ¼ cup apple cider vinegar

- 2 tablespoons coconut aminos

Directions:

1. In your slow cooker, mix beans with maple syrup, BBQ sauce, stevia, water, tomato paste, mustard, oil, vinegar and aminos, stir, cover and cook on Low for 12 hours.

2. Divide into bowls and serve hot.

3. Enjoy!

Nutrition:

Calories 576,
Fat 18.5,
Fiber 3,
Carbs 29.43,
Protein 23

Squash Chili

Preparation time: 10 minutes
Cooking time: 6 hours
Servings: 8
Ingredients:

- 2 carrots, chopped

- 1 yellow onion, chopped

- 2 celery stalks, chopped

- 2 green apples, cored, peeled and chopped

- 4 garlic cloves, minced

- 2 cups butternut squash, peeled and cubed

- 6 ounces canned chickpeas, drained

- 6 ounces canned black beans, drained

- 7 ounces canned coconut milk

- 2 teaspoons chili powder

- 1 teaspoon oregano, dried

- 1 tablespoon cumin, ground

- 2 cups veggie stock

- 2 tablespoons tomato paste

- Salt and black pepper to the taste

- 1 tablespoon cilantro, chopped

Directions:

1. In your slow cooker, mix carrots with onion, celery, apples, garlic, squash, chickpeas, black beans, coconut milk, chili powder, oregano, cumin, stock, tomato paste, salt and pepper, stir, cover and cook on High for 6 hours.

2. Add cilantro, stir, divide into bowls and serve.

3. Enjoy!

Nutrition:

Calories 376,

Fat 18.5,

Fiber 3,

Carbs 29.43,

Protein 23

Rich Lentils Soup

Preparation time: 10 minutes
Cooking time: 2 hours and 30 minutes
Servings: 4
Ingredients:

- 2 teaspoons garlic, minced

- 1 tablespoon olive oil

- 1 yellow onion, chopped

- 1 teaspoon cumin, ground

- 1 teaspoon coriander seeds

- 1 teaspoon turmeric powder

- 1 teaspoon cinnamon powder

- ½ teaspoon garam masala

- 1 and ½ cups red lentils

- 4 cups veggie stock

- 14 ounces coconut milk

- 4 cups spinach

- Salt and black pepper to the taste

Directions:

1. In your slow cooker, mix garlic with oil, onion, cumin, coriander, turmeric, cinnamon, garam

masala, lentils and stock, stir, cover and cook on High for 2 hours.

2. Add coconut, spinach, salt and pepper, stir and cook on High for 30 minutes more.

3. Ladle into bowls and serve.

4. Enjoy!

Nutrition:
Calories 176,
Fat 18.5,
Fiber 3,
Carbs 29.43,
Protein 23

Easy Lentils Mix

Preparation time: 10 minutes
Cooking time: 4 hours and 30 minutes
Servings: 6
Ingredients:

- 6 cups sweet potatoes, cubed

- 1 yellow onion, chopped

- 3 cups veggie stock

- 2 teaspoons coriander, ground

- 4 garlic cloves, minced

- 2 teaspoons chili powder

- 2 teaspoons garam masala

- 1 and ½ cups red lentils

- 8 ounces canned coconut milk

- 1 cup water

- A pinch of salt and black pepper to the taste

Directions:
1. In your slow cooker, mix potatoes with onion, stock, coriander, garlic, chili powder, garam masala, salt and pepper, stir, cover and cook on High for 3 hours.

2. Add lentils and water, stir, cover and cook on High for 1 hour and 30 minutes more.

3. Add coconut milk, more salt and pepper if needed, stir, cover, leave aside for a few minutes, divide between plates and serve.

4. Enjoy!

Nutrition:
Calories 176,
Fat 18.5,
Fiber 3,
Carbs 29.43,
Protein 23

Quinoa and Beans Chili

Preparation time: 10 minutes
Cooking time: 3 hours
Servings: 4
Ingredients:

- 15 ounces canned black beans, drained

- 2 and ¼ cups veggie stock

- ½ cup quinoa

- 14 ounces canned tomatoes, chopped

- ¼ cup red bell pepper, chopped

- 1 carrot, shredded

- ¼ cup green bell pepper, chopped

- 2 garlic cloves, minced

- ½ chili pepper, chopped

- 2 teaspoons chili powder

- 1 small yellow onion, chopped

- A pinch of salt and black pepper

- 1 teaspoon oregano, dried

- 1 teaspoon cumin, ground

- ½ cup corn

For the cashew cream:

- 4 tablespoons water

- ½ cup cashews, soaked overnight and drained

- A pinch of salt and black pepper

- A drizzle of white vinegar

- 1 teaspoon lime juice

Directions:

1. In your slow cooker, mix black beans with stock, quinoa, tomatoes, red and green bell pepper, carrot, garlic, chili, chili powder, onion, salt, pepper, oregano, cumin and corn, stir, cover and cook on High for 3 hours.

2. Meanwhile, in your blender, mix cashews with water, salt, pepper, vinegar and lime juice and pulse really well.

3. Divide chili into bowls, spread cashew cream on top and serve.

4. Enjoy!

Nutrition:

Calories 376,
Fat 18.5,
Fiber 3,
Carbs 29.43,
Protein 23

Potatoes and Spinach Mix

Preparation time: 10 minutes
Cooking time: 3 hours
Servings: 4
Ingredients:

- 1 pound potatoes, cubed

- 1 small onion, chopped

- 2 tablespoons water

- 1 tablespoon olive oil

- ½ teaspoon cumin, ground

- ½ teaspoon coriander, ground

- ½ teaspoon garam masala

- ½ teaspoon chili powder

- ½ pound spinach, torn

- Black pepper to the taste

Directions:

1. In your slow cooker, mix potatoes with onion, water, oil, cumin, coriander, garam masala, chili, spinach and black pepper, stir, cover and cook on High for 3 hours.

2. Divide into bowls and serve.

3. Enjoy!

Nutrition:

Calories 276,

Fat 18.5,

Fiber 3,

Carbs 29.43,

Protein 23

Rich White Bean Soup

Preparation time: 10 minutes

Cooking time: 4 hours

Servings: 6

Ingredients:

- 1 pounds navy beans, dried

- 1 yellow onion, chopped

- 2 quarts veggie stock

- Salt and black pepper to the taste

- 2 potatoes, cubed

- 1 pound carrots, sliced

- 1 cup sun-dried tomatoes, chopped

- 2 teaspoons dill, chopped

- 4 tablespoons parsley, chopped

Directions:

1. In your slow cooker, mix beans with onion, stock, salt, pepper, potatoes, carrots, tomatoes, dill and parsley, stir, cover and cook on High for 4 hours.

2. Ladle into bowls and serve.

3. Enjoy!

Nutrition:

Calories 376,
Fat 18.5,
Fiber 3,
Carbs 29.43,
Protein 23

Intense Tofu and Pineapple Mix

Preparation time: 10 minutes
Cooking time: 10 hours
Servings: 5
Ingredients:

- 2 pounds firm tofu, pressed and cut into medium rectangles
- 1 tablespoons sesame oil
- 3 tablespoons coconut aminos
- ½ cup veggie stock
- 1 cup pineapple juice
- ¼ cup rice vinegar
- 2 tablespoons stevia
- 1 tablespoon ginger, grated
- 3 garlic cloves, minced
- 6 pineapple rings

Directions:

1. In your slow cooker, mix tofu with sesame oil, coconut aminos, stock, pineapple juice, vinegar, stevia, ginger, garlic and pineapple rings, stir, cover and cook on Low for 10 hours.

2. Divide into bowls and serve.

3. Enjoy!

Nutrition:
Calories 126,
Fat 18.5,
Fiber 3,
Carbs 29.43,
Protein 23

Vegan Jambalaya

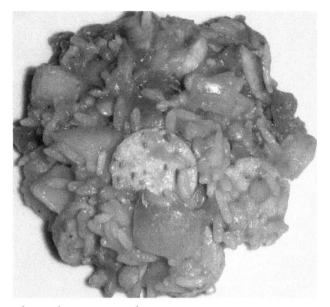

Preparation time: 10 minutes
Cooking time: 4 hours
Servings: 6
Ingredients:

- 1 green bell pepper, chopped

- 1 cup okra

- 1 small yellow onion, chopped

- 2 garlic cloves, minced

- 3 celery ribs, chopped

- 16 ounces canned tomatoes, chopped

- 1 and ½ cups veggie stock

- ½ teaspoon paprika

- A pinch of salt and black pepper

Directions:

1. In your slow cooker, mix bell pepper with okra, onion, garlic, celery, tomatoes, stock, paprika, salt and pepper, stir, cover and cook on Low for 4 hours.

2. Divide into bowls and serve.

Enjoy!

Nutrition:

Calories 376,

Fat 18.5,

Fiber 3,

Carbs 29.43,

Protein 23

Pork Chops

Preparation time: 5 minutes

Cooking time: 6 hours

Servings: 8

Ingredients:

- 2 pounds pasture-raised pork chops

- 1 teaspoon salt

- 1 tablespoon dried thyme

- 1 tablespoon dried rosemary

- 1 tablespoon ground cumin

- 1 tablespoon dried curry powder

- 1 tablespoon chopped fresh chives

- 1 tablespoon fennel seeds

- 1 tablespoons avocado oil

Directions:

1   Place 2 tablespoons oil in a small bowl, add remaining **Ingredients:** except for pork, and stir until well mixed.

2   Rub this mixture on all sides of pork chops until evenly coated.

3   Grease a 6-quart slow cooker with remaining oil, add seasoned pork chops, and shut with lid.

4   Plug in the slow cooker and cook pork for 6 hours at a low heat setting or 4 hours at a high heat setting.

5   Serve straight away.

Nutrition:

Net Carbs: 1g

Calories: 235

Total Fat: 15g

Saturated Fat: 3g

Protein: 24g

Carbs: 1g

Fiber: 0g

Sugar: 0g

Spicy Pork & Spinach Stew

Preparation time: 5 minutes

Cooking time: 4 hours and 20 minutes

Servings: 5

Ingredients:

• 1-pound pasture-raised pork butt, fat trimmed and cut into 2-inch pieces

• 4 cups chopped baby spinach

• 4 ounces Rotel tomatoes

• 1 large white onion, peeled and quartered

• cloves of garlic, peeled

• 1 teaspoon dried thyme

• 2 teaspoons Cajun seasoning blend

• 2 tablespoons avocado oil

- ¾ cup heavy whipping cream

Directions:

1   Place tomatoes, onion, and garlic in a food processor and pulse for 1 to 2 minutes or until blended.

2   Pour this mixture into a 6-quart slow cooker, add Cajun seasoning mix, thyme, avocado oil, and pork pieces, and stir well until evenly coated.

3   Plug in the slow cooker, then shut with lid and cook for 5 hours at low heat setting or 2 hours at high heat setting.

4   When done, stir in cream until combined, add spinach and continue cooking at low heat setting for 20 minutes or more until spinach wilts.

5   Serve straight away.

Nutrition:

Net Carbs: 3.3g

Calories: 604

Total Fat: 38.3g

Saturated Fat: 9g

Protein: 56g

Carbs: 9g

Fiber: 5g;

Sugar: 4g

Stuffed Taco Peppers

Preparation time: 5 minutes

Cooking time: 8 hours

Servings: 6

Ingredients:

- 1 cup cauliflower rice

- 1 small red bell peppers

- 18-ounce minced pork, pasture-raised

- 1 teaspoon garlic powder

- ¾ teaspoon salt

- 1 teaspoon red chili powder

- 1 cup shredded Monterey jack cheese and more for topping

- 2 tablespoons avocado oil

- 1 cup water

Directions:

1   Remove and discard stem from each pepper and then scoop out seeds.

2   Place meat in a large bowl, add garlic, salt, and red chili powder, and stir until combined.

3   Then stir in cauliflower rice and oil until just combine and then stir in cheese.

4   Stuff this mixture into each pepper and place them in a 4-quart slow cooker.

5   Pour water into the bottom of the slow cooker, switch it on, and shut with the lid.

6   Cook peppers for 4 hours at high heat setting or 8 hours at low heating setting and top peppers with more cheese in the last 10 minutes of cooking time.

7   Serve straight away.

Nutrition:

Net Carbs: 4g

Calories: 270

Total Fat: 18g

Saturated Fat: 5g

Protein: 21g

Carbs: 6g

Fiber: 2g

Sugar: 3g

Lamb Barbacoa

Preparation time: 5 minutes

Cooking time: 8 hours

Servings: 12

Ingredients:

- 2 pounds pasture-raised pork shoulder, fat trimmed

- 2 tablespoons salt

- 1 teaspoon chipotle powder

- 2 tablespoons smoked paprika

- 1 tablespoon ground cumin

- 1 tablespoon dried oregano

- ¼ cup dried mustard

- 1 cup water

Directions:

1   Stir together salt, chipotle powder, paprika, cumin, oregano, and mustard and rub this mixture generously all over the pork.

2   Place seasoned pork into a 6-quart slow cooker, plug it in, then shut with lid and cook for 6 hours at high heat setting.

3   When done, shred pork with two forks and stir well until coated well.

4   Serve straight away.

Nutrition:

Net Carbs: 0.7g

Calories: 477

Total Fat: 35.8g

Saturated Fat: 14.8g

Protein: 37.5g

Carbs: 1.2g

Fiber: 0.5g

Sugar: 5g

Pork Chile Verde

Preparation time: 5 minutes

Cooking time: 7 hours and 5 minutes

Servings: 6

Ingredients:

- 2 pounds pasture-raised pork shoulder, cut into 6 pieces

- 1 teaspoon sea salt

- ½ teaspoon ground black pepper

- 1 ½ tablespoon avocado oil

- 1 ½ cup salsa Verde

- 1 cup chicken broth

Directions:

1   Season pork with salt and black pepper.

2   Place a large skillet pan over medium heat, add oil, and when hot, add seasoned pork pieces.

3   Cook pork for 3 to 4 minutes per side or until browned and then transfer to a 6-quart slow cooker.

4   Whisk together salsa and chicken broth and pour over pork pieces.

5   Plug in the slow cooker, then shut with lid and cook for 6 to 7 hours at low heat setting or until pork is very tender.

6   When done, shred pork with two forks and stir until combined.

Nutrition :

Net Carbs: 4g

Calories : 342

Total Fat: 22g

Saturated Fat: 12g

Protein: 32g

Carbs: 6g

Fiber: 2g

Sugar: 4g

Ham Soup

Preparation time: 5 minutes

Cooking time: 4 hours

Servings: 6

Ingredients:

- 2 pounds pasture-raised smoked ham hock

- 2 cups cauliflower florets

- 2 bay leaves

- ¼ teaspoon nutmeg

- cups bone broth

Directions:

1   Place cauliflower florets in a 6-quarts slow cooker, add remaining Ingredients, and pour in water until all the Ingredients are just submerged.

2   Plug in the slow cooker, then shut with lid and cook for 4 hours at high heat setting or until cauliflower florets are very tender.

3   Transfer ham to a bowl, shred with two forms, and discard bone and fat pieces.

4   Puree cauliflower in the slow cooker with a stick blender for 1 to 2 minutes or until smooth, return shredded ham, and stir until well combined.

5   Taste soup to adjust seasoning and serve.

Nutrition :

Net Carbs: 3g

Calories : 349

Total Fat: 23g

Saturated Fat: 10g

Protein: 34g

Carbs: 5g

Fiber: 2g

Sugar: 2g

Minced Pork Zucchini Lasagna

Preparation time: 20 minutes

Cooking time: 8 hours

Servings: 4

Ingredients:

- medium zucchinis

- 1 diced small onion

- 1 minced clove of garlic

- 2 cups of minced lean ground pork

- 2 cans of Italian diced tomatoes

- 2 tablespoons of olive oil

- 2 cups of shredded Mozzarella cheese

- 1 large egg

- 1 tablespoon of dried basil

- Salt and pepper

- 2 tablespoons of butter

Directions:

1   Slice the zucchini lengthwise into 6 slices.

2   Heat the olive oil in a saucepan, and sauté the garlic and onions for 5 minutes.

3   Add the minced meat and cook for a further 5 minutes.

4   Add the tomatoes and cook for a further 5 minutes.

5   Add the seasoning and mix thoroughly.

6   In a small bowl, combine the egg and cheese and whisk together.

7   Use the butter to grease the crock pot and then begin to layer the lasagna.

8   First, layer with the zucchini slices, add the meat mixture, and then top with the cheese.

9   Repeat and finish with the cheese.

10   Cover and cook for 8 hours on low.

Nutrition:

Carbohydrates: 10 grams

Protein: 23 grams

Fat: 30 grams

Calories: 398

Beef Dijon

Preparation time: 15 minutes

Cooking time: 5 hours

Servings: 4

Ingredients:

- (6 oz.) small round steaks

- 2 tbsp. of each:

- Steak seasoning - to taste

- Avocado oil

- Peanut oil

- Balsamic vinegar/dry sherry

- tbsp. large chopped green onions/small chopped onions for the garnish - extra

- 1/4 c. whipping cream

- 1 c. fresh crimini mushrooms - sliced

- 1 tbsp. Dijon mustard

Directions:

1   Warm up the oils using the high heat setting on the stove top. Flavor each of the steaks with pepper and arrange to a skillet.

2   Cook two to three minutes per side until done.

3   Place into the slow cooker. Pour in the skillet drippings, half of the mushrooms, and the onions.

4   Cook on the low setting for four hours.

5   When the cooking time is done, scoop out the onions, mushrooms, and steaks to a serving platter.

6   In a separate dish - whisk together the mustard, balsamic vinegar, whipping cream, and the steak drippings from the slow cooker.

7   Empty the gravy into a gravy server and pour over the steaks.

8   Enjoy with some brown rice, riced cauliflower, or potatoes.

Nutrition:

Calories: 535

Net Carbs: 5.0 g

Fat: 40 g

Protein: 39 g

Cabbage & Corned Beef

Preparation time: 10 minutes

Cooking time: 8 hours

Servings: 10

Ingredients:

- lb. corned beef

- 1 large head of cabbage

- c. water

- 1 celery bunch

- 1 small onion

- 4 carrots

- ½ t. of each:

- Ground mustard

- Ground coriander

- Ground marjoram

- Black pepper

- Salt

- Ground thyme

- Allspice

Directions:

1   Dice the carrots, onions, and celery and toss them into the cooker. Pour in the water.

2   Combine the spices, rub the beef, and arrange in the cooker. Secure the lid and cook on low for seven hours.

3   Remove the top layer of cabbage. Wash and cut it into quarters it until ready to cook. When the beef is done, add the cabbage, and cook for one hour on the low setting.

4   Serve and enjoy.

Nutrition:

Calories: 583

Net Carbs: 13 g

Fat: 40 g

Protein: 42 g

Chipotle Barbacoa

Preparation time: 20 minutes

Cooking time: 4 hours

Servings: 9

Ingredients:

- ½ c. beef/chicken broth

- 2 med. chilies in adobo (with the sauce, it's about 4 teaspoons)

- lb. chuck roast/beef brisket

- minced garlic cloves

- 2 tbsp. of each:

- Lime juice

- Apple cider vinegar

- 2 t. of each:

- Sea salt

- Cumin

- 1 tbsp. dried oregano

- 1 t. black pepper

- 2 whole bay leaves

- Optional: ½ t. ground cloves

Directions:

1   Mix the chilies in the sauce, and add the broth, garlic, ground cloves, pepper, cumin, salt, vinegar, and lime juice in a blender, mixing until smooth.

2   Chop the beef into two-inch chunks and toss it in the slow cooker. Empty the puree on top. Toss in the two bay leaves.

3   Cook four to six hrs. On the high setting or eight to ten using the low setting.

4   Dispose of the bay leaves when the meat is done.

5   Shred and stir into the juices to simmer for five to ten minutes.

Nutrition:

Calories: 242

Net Carbs: 2 g

Fat: 11 g

Protein: 32 g

Corned Beef Cabbage Rolls

Preparation time: 25 minutes

Cooking time: 6 hours

Servings: 5

Ingredients:

- ½ lb. corned beef

- large savoy cabbage leaves

- ¼ c. of each:

- White wine

- Coffee

- 1 large lemon

- 1 med. sliced onion

- 1 tbsp. of each:

- Rendered bacon fat

- Erythritol

- Yellow mustard

2 t. of each:

- Kosher salt

- Worcestershire sauce

¼ t. of each:

- Cloves

- Allspice

- 1 large bay leaf

1 t. of each:

- Mustard seeds

- Whole peppercorns

- ½ t. red pepper flakes

Directions:

1   Add the liquids, spices, and corned beef into the cooker. Cook six hours on the low setting.

2   Prepare a pot of boiling water.

3   When the time is up, add the leaves along with the sliced onion to the water for two to three minutes.

4   Transfer the leaves to a cold-water bath - blanching them for three to four minutes. Continue boiling the onion.

5   Use a paper towel to dry the leaves. Add the onions and beef. Roll up the cabbage leaves.

6   Drizzle with freshly squeezed lemon juice.

Nutrition:

Calories: 481.4

Net Carbs: 4.2 g

Protéine: 34.87 g

Fat: 25.38 g

Cube Steak

Preparation time: 15 minutes

Cooking time: 8 hours

Servings: 8

Ingredients:

- Cubed steaks (28 oz.)

- 1 ¾ t. adobo seasoning/garlic salt

- 1 can (8 oz.) tomato sauce

- 1 c. water

- Black pepper to taste

- ½ med. onion

- 1 small red pepper

- 1/3 c. green pitted olives (+) 2 tbsp. brine

Directions:

1   Slice the peppers and onions into ¼-inch strips.

2   Sprinkle the steaks with the pepper and garlic salt as needed and place them in the cooker.

3   Fold in the peppers and onion along with the water, sauce, and olives (with the liquid/brine from the jar).

4   Close the lid. Prepare using the low-temperature setting for eight hours.

Nutrition :

Calories : 154

Net Carbs: 4 g

Protein: 23.5 g

Fat: 5.5 g

Ragu

Preparation time: 10 minutes

Cooking time: 8 hours

Servings: 2

Ingredients:

- ¼ of each - diced:

- 4 Carrot

- Rib of celery

- 1 Onion

- 1 minced garlic clove

- ½ lb. top-round lean beef

(3 oz.) Of each:

- Diced tomatoes

- Crushed tomatoes

- 2 ½ t. beef broth (+) ¼ c.

1 ¼ t. of each:

- Chopped fresh thyme

- Minced fresh rosemary

- 1 bay leaf

- Pepper & Salt to taste

Directions:

1   Place the prepared celery, garlic, onion, and carrots into the slow cooker.

2   Trim away the fat and add the meat to the slow cooker. Sprinkle with the salt and pepper

3   Stir in the rest of the Ingredient.

4   Prepare on the low setting for six to eight hours. Enjoy any way you choose.

Nutrition:

Calories: 224

Net Carbs: 6 g

Protein: 27 g

Fat: 9 g

Rope Vieja

Preparation time: 15 minutes

Cooking time: 8 hours

Servings: 6

Ingredients:

- 2 lb. flank steak – remove fat

1 of each:

- Yellow pepper

- Thinly sliced onion

- Green pepper

- Bay leaf

- ¼ t. salt

¾ t. of each:

- Oregano

- Non-fat beef broth

- Tomato paste

- Cooking spray

Directions:

1   Prepare the slow cooker with the spray or use a liner and combine all of the fixings.

2   Stir everything together and prepare using low for eight hours.

3   Top it off with your chosen garnishes.

Nutrition:

Calories: 257

Net Carbs: 7 g

Fat: 10 g

Protein: 35 g

Spinach Soup

Preparation time: 15 minutes

Cooking time: 6-8 hours

Servings: 4

Ingredients:

- 2 pounds spinach

- ¼ cup cream cheese

- 1 onion, diced

- 2 cups heavy cream

- 1 garlic clove, minced

- 2 cups water

- salt, pepper, to taste

Directions:

1   Pour water into the slow cooker. Add spinach, salt, and pepper.

2   Add cream cheese, onion, garlic, and heavy cream.

3   Close the lid and cook on Low for 6-8 hours.

4   Puree soup with blender and serve.

Nutrition:

Calories 322

Fats 28.2g

Net carbs 10.1g

Protein 12.2g

Mashed Cauliflower with Herbs

Preparation time: 15 minutes

Cooking time: 3-6 hours

Servings: 4

Ingredients:

- 1 cauliflower head, cut into florets

- garlic cloves, peeled

- ½ teaspoon fresh rosemary, chopped

- ½ teaspoon fresh thyme, chopped

- ½ teaspoon fresh sage, chopped

- ½ teaspoon fresh parsley, chopped

- 1 cup vegetable broth

- 2 cups water

- 1 tablespoons ghee

- Salt, pepper, to taste

Directions:

1   Pour broth into the slow cooker, add cauliflower florets.

2   Add water, it should cover the cauliflower.

3   Close the lid and cook on Low for 6 hours or on High for 3 hours.

4   Once cooked, drain water from the slow cooker.

5   Add herbs, salt, and pepper, and ghee, puree with a blender.

Nutrition:

Calories 115

Fats 12g

Net carbs 4.7g

Protein 6.2g

Kale Quiche

Preparation time: 15 minutes

Cooking time: 3-5 hours

Servings: 3

Ingredients:

- 1 cup almond milk

- 4 eggs

- 1 cup Carbquick Baking Mix

- 2 cups spinach, chopped

- ½ bell pepper, chopped

- cups fresh baby kale, chopped

- 1 teaspoon garlic, chopped

- 1/3 cup fresh basil, chopped

- salt, pepper, to taste

- 1 tablespoon olive oil

Directions:

1	Add oil to a slow cooker or use a cooking spray.

2	Beat eggs into a slow cooker; add almond milk and Baking Mix, mix to combine.

3	Add spinach, bell pepper, garlic, and basil, stir to combine.

4	Close the lid and cook on Low for 5 hours or on High for 3 hours.

5	Make sure the quiche is done, check the center with a toothpick, it should be dry.

Nutrition :

Calories 273

Fats 24.4g

Net carbs 5.8g

Protein 10.5g

Spinach Stuffed Portobello

Preparation time: 15 minutes

Cooking time: 3 hours

Servings: 8

Ingredients:

- oz. medium-sized Portobello mushrooms, stems removed

- 1 tablespoons olive oil

- ½ onion, chopped

- 2 cups fresh spinach, rinsed and chopped

- garlic cloves, minced

- 1 cup chicken broth

- tablespoons parmesan cheese, grated

- 1/3 teaspoon dried thyme

- salt, pepper, to taste

Directions:

1   Heat oil in a medium pan over high heat. Add onion, cook until translucent, stirring steadily. Add spinach and thyme, cook for 1-2 minutes until spinach is wilted.

2   Brush each mushroom with olive oil.

3   Put 1 tablespoon of onion and spinach stuffing into each mushroom.

4   Pour chicken broth into a slow cooker. Put stuffed mushrooms on the bottom.

5   Close the lid and cook on High for 3 hours.

6   Once cooked, sprinkle mushrooms with parmesan cheese and serve.

Nutrition:

Calories 310g

Fats 21g

Net carbs 3g

Protein 12g

Poached Salmon

Preparation time: 15 minutes

Cooking time: 1 hour

Servings: 4

Ingredients:

- medium salmon fillets

- water

- 2 tablespoons dry white wine

- 1 yellow onion, sliced

- ½ lemon, sliced

- ½ teaspoon salt

- ¼ teaspoon garlic powder

- ¼ teaspoon dried basil

Directions:

1   Pour water and wine into a slow cooker. Heat on High for 30 minutes with the lid open.

2   Season salmon fillets with salt, garlic powder, and basil.

3   Put salmon into a slow cooker. Add onion and lemon onto salmon fillets.

4   Close the lid and cook on High for 20-30 minutes.

Nutrition :

Calories 273

Fats 21g

Net carbs 4.2g

Protein 35g

Cod and Vegetables

Preparation time: 15 minutes

Cooking time: 1-3 hours

Servings: 4

Ingredients:

- (5-6 oz.) cod fillets

- 1 bell pepper, sliced or chopped

- 1 onion, sliced

- ½ fresh lemon, sliced

- 1 zucchini, sliced

- garlic cloves, minced

- ¼ cup low-sodium broth

- 1 teaspoon rosemary

- ¼ teaspoon red pepper flakes

- Salt, pepper, to taste

Directions:

1   Season cod fillets with salt and pepper.

2   Pour broth into a slow cooker, add garlic, rosemary, bell pepper, onion, and zucchini into the slow cooker.

3   Put fish into your slow cooker, add lemon slices on top.

4   Close the lid and cook on Low for 2-3 hours or on High for 1 hour.

Nutrition:

Calories 150

Fats 11.6g

Net carbs 6.2g

Protein 26.9g

Balsamic Beef Pot Roast

Preparation time: 15 minutes

Cooking time: 4 hours

Servings: 10

Ingredients:

- 1 boneless (3 lb.) chuck roast

- 1 tbsp. of each:

- Kosher salt

- Black ground pepper

- Garlic powder

- ¼ c. balsamic vinegar

- ½ c. chopped onion

- 2 c. water

- ¼ t. xanthan gum

- For the Garnish: Fresh parsley

Directions:

1   Season the chuck roast with garlic powder, pepper, and salt over the entire surface.

2   Use a large skillet to sear the roast until browned.

3   Deglaze the bottom of the pot using balsamic vinegar. Cook one minute. Add to the slow cooker.

4   Mix in the onion and add the water. Once it starts to boil, secure the lid, and continue cooking on low for three to four hours.

5   Take the meat out of the slow cooker, and place it in a large bowl where you will break it up carefully into large chunks.

6   Remove all fat and anything else that may not be healthy such as too much fat.

7   Whisk the xanthan gum into the broth, and add it back to the slow cooker.

8   Serve and enjoy with a smile!

Nutrition :

Calories : 393

Net Carbs: 3 g

Protein: 30 g

Moist and Spicy Pulled Chicken Breast

Preparation time: 15 minutes
Cooking time: 6 hours
Servings: 8
Ingredients:

- 1 teaspoon dry oregano
- 1 teaspoon dry thyme
- 1 teaspoon dried rosemary
- 1 teaspoon garlic powder
- 1 teaspoon sweet paprika
- ½ teaspoon chili powder
- Salt and pepper to taste
- tablespoons butter
- pounds of chicken breasts
- 1 ½ cups ready-made tomato salsa
- 2 Tablespoons of olive oil

Directions:

1. Mix dry seasoning, sprinkle half on the bottom of slow cooker.
2. Place the chicken breasts over it, sprinkle the rest of the spices.
3. Pour the salsa over the chicken. Cover, cook on low for 6 hours.

Nutrition:

Calories: 42

Carbs: 1g

Fat: 1g

Protein: 9g

Whole Roasted Chicken

Preparation time: 15 minutes
Cooking time: 8 hours
Servings: 6
Ingredients:

- 1 whole chicken (approximately 5.5 pounds)
- garlic cloves
- small onions
- 1 Tablespoon olive oil, for rubbing
- 2 teaspoons salt
- 2 teaspoons sweet paprika
- 1 teaspoon Cayenne pepper
- 1 teaspoon onion powder
- 1 teaspoon ground thyme
- 2 teaspoons fresh ground black pepper
- Tablespoons butter, cut into cubes

Directions:

1. Mix all dry **Ingredients:** well.
2. Stuff the chicken belly with garlic and onions.
3. On the bottom of the slow cooker, place four balls of aluminum foil.
4. Set the chicken on top of the balls. Rub it generously with olive oil.
5. Cover the chicken with seasoning, drop in butter pieces. Cover, cook on low for 8 hours.

Nutrition:

Calories: 120

Carbs: 1g

Fat: 6g

Protein: 17g

Pot Roast Beef Brisket

Preparation time: 15 minutes
Cooking time: 12 hours
Servings: 10
Ingredients:

- o pounds beef brisket, whole
- 2 Tablespoons olive oil
- 2 Tablespoons apple cider vinegar
- 1 teaspoon dry oregano
- 1 teaspoon dry thyme
- 1 teaspoon dried rosemary
- 2 Tablespoons paprika
- 1 teaspoon Cayenne pepper
- 1 tablespoon salt
- 1 teaspoon fresh ground black pepper

Directions:

1. In a bowl, mix dry seasoning, add olive oil, apple cider vinegar.
2. Place the meat in the slow cooker, generously coat with seasoning mix.
3. Cover, cook on low for 12 hours.
4. Remove the brisket, place it on a pan. Sear it under the broiler for 2-4 minutes, observe it, so the meat doesn't burn.
5. Wrap it using a foil, then let it rest for 1 hour. Slice and serve.

Nutrition:
Calories: 280
Carbs: 4g

Fat: 20g
Protein: 20g

Seriously Delicious Lamb Roast

Preparation time: 15 minutes
Cooking time: 8 hours
Servings: 8
Ingredients:

- medium radishes, scrubbed, washed, and cut in half
- Salt and pepper to taste
- 1 red onion, diced
- 2 garlic cloves, minced
- 1 lamb joint (approximately 4.5 pounds) at room temperature
- 2 Tablespoons olive oil
- 1 teaspoon dry oregano
- 1 teaspoon dry thyme
- 1 sprig fresh rosemary
- cups heated broth, your choice

Directions:

1. Place cut radishes along the bottom of the slow cooker. Season. Add onion and garlic.
2. Blend the herbs plus olive oil in a small bowl until it forms to paste.
3. Place the meat on top of the radishes. Knead the paste over the meat.
4. Heat the stock, pour it around the meat.
5. Cover, cook on low for 8 hours. Let it rest for 20 minutes. Slice and serve.

Nutrition:
Calories: 206

Carbs: 4g
Fat: 9g
Protein: 32g

Lamb Provençal

Preparation time: 15 minutes

Cooking time: 8 hours

Servings: 4

Ingredients:

- 2 racks lamb, approximately 2 pounds
- 1 Tablespoon olive oil
- 2 Tablespoons fresh rosemary, chopped
- 1 Tablespoon fresh thyme, chopped
- garlic cloves, minced
- 1 teaspoon dry oregano
- 1 lemon, the zest
- 1 teaspoon minced fresh ginger
- 1 cup (Good) red wine
- Salt and pepper to taste

Directions:

1. Preheat the slow cooker on low.
2. In a pan, heat 1 tablespoon olive oil. Brown the meat for 2 minutes per side.
3. Mix remaining **Ingredients:** in a bowl.
4. Place the lamb in the slow cooker, pour the remaining seasoning over the meat.
5. Cover, cook on low for 8 hours.

Nutrition:

Calories: 140

Carbs: 3g

Fat: 5g

Protein: 21g

Greek Style Lamb Shanks

Preparation time: 15 minutes
Cooking time: 6 hours
Servings: 8
Ingredients:

- Tablespoons butter
- lamb shanks, approximately 1 pound each
- 2 Tablespoons olive oil
- 8-10 pearl onions
- garlic cloves, minced
- 2 beef tomatoes, cubed
- ¼ cup of green olives
- bay leaves
- 1 sprig fresh rosemary
- 1 teaspoon dry thyme
- 1 teaspoon ground cumin
- 1 cup fresh spinach
- ¾ cup hot water
- ½ cup red wine, Merlot or Cabernet
- Salt and pepper to taste

Directions:

1. Liquify the butter in a pan, then cook the shanks on each side.
2. Remove, then add oil, onions, garlic. Cook for 3-4 minutes. Add tomatoes, olives, spices, then stir well. Put the liquids and return the meat. Boil for 1 minute.
3. Transfer everything to the slow cooker.
4. Cover, cook on medium-high for 6 hours.

Nutrition:

Calories: 250

Carbs: 3g

Fat: 16g

Protein: 22g

Homemade Meatballs and Spaghetti Squash

Preparation time: 15 minutes
Cooking time: 8 hours
Servings: 8
Ingredients:

- 1 medium-sized spaghetti squash, washed, halved
- 1 Tablespoon butter, to grease the slow cooker
    - pounds lean ground beef
- 2 garlic cloves
- 1 red onion, chopped
- ½ cup almond flour
- 2 Tablespoons of dry Parmesan cheese
- 1 egg, beaten
- 1 teaspoon ground cumin
- Salt and pepper to taste
- cans diced Italian tomatoes
- 1 small can tomato paste, 28 ounces
- 1 cup hot water
- 1 red onion, chopped
- ¼ cup chopped parsley
- ½ teaspoon each, salt and sugar (optional)
- 1 bay leaf

Directions:

1   Grease the slow cooker, place both squash halves open side down in the slow cooker.

2   Mix meatball **Ingredients:** in a bowl—form approximately 20 small meatballs.

3   In a pan, heat the olive oil. Fry the meatballs within 2-3 minutes per side. Transfer to the slow cooker.

4   In the small bowl, add the tomatoes, tomato paste, oil, water, onion, and parsley, add ½ teaspoon each of salt and sugar. Mix well.

5   Pour the marinara sauce in the slow cooker around the squash halves.

6   Cover, cook on low for 8 hours.

Nutrition:

Calories: 235

Carbs: 12g

Fat: 14g

Protein: 15g

Beef and Cabbage Roast

Preparation time: 15 minutes

Cooking time: 8 hours

Servings: 10

Ingredients:

- 1 red onion, quartered
- 2 garlic cloves, minced
- 2-3 stocks celery, diced (approximately 1 cup)
- 4-6 dry pimento berries
- 2 bay leaves
  - pounds beef brisket (two pieces)

- 1 teaspoon chili powder
- 1 teaspoon ground cumin
- 2 cups broth, beef + 2 cups hot water
- Salt and pepper to taste
- 1 medium cabbage (approximately 2.2 pounds), cut in half, then quartered

Directions:

1 Add all Ingredients, except cabbage, to the slow cooker in order of the list.
2 Cover, cook on low for 7 hours.
3 Uncover, add the cabbage on top of the stew. Re-cover, cook for 1 additional hour.

Nutrition:

Calories: 150

Carbs: 8g

Fat: 3g

Protein: 22g

Simple Chicken Chili

Preparation time: 15 minutes
Cooking time: 6 hours
Servings: 8
Ingredients:

- 1 Tablespoon butter
- 1 red onion, sliced
- 1 bell pepper, sliced
- 2 garlic cloves, minced
- pounds boneless chicken thighs
- slices bacon, chopped
- 1 teaspoon chili powder
- Salt and pepper to taste
- 1 cup chicken broth
- ¼ cup of coconut milk
- Tablespoons tomato paste

Directions:

1. Add all **Ingredients:** to the slow cooker, starting with the butter.
2. Cover, cook on low for 6 hours.
3. Strip the chicken using a fork in the slow cooker. Serve.

Nutrition:

Calories: 210
Carbs: 32g
Fat: 4g
Protein: 14g

Beef Shoulder in BBQ Sauce

Preparation time: 15 minutes
Cooking time: 10 hours
Servings: 12
Ingredients:

- pounds beef shoulder, whole
- 1 Tablespoon butter
- 1 yellow onion, diced
- 1 garlic bulb, peeled and minced
- Tablespoons red wine vinegar
- 2 Tablespoons Worcestershire sauce
- Tablespoons Swerve (or a suitable substitute)
- 1 Tablespoon mustard
- 1 teaspoon salt
- 1 teaspoon fresh ground black pepper

Directions:

1   In a bowl, mix seasoning. Set aside.
2   Liquify the butter in a pan, add the meat. Brown on all sides. Transfer to slow cooker.
3   Fry the onion within 2-3 minutes in the same pan, then pour over the meat.
4   Pour in the seasoning. Cover, cook on low for 10 hours.
5   Remove, cover it with foil, and then let it rest for 1 hour.
6   Turn the slow cooker on high, reduce the remaining liquid by half and serve with the shredded beef.

Nutrition:

Calories: 140

Carbs: 5g
Fat: 9g
Protein: 8g

Dressed Pork Leg Roast

Preparation time: 15 minutes
Cooking time: 8 hours
Servings: 14
Ingredients:

- pounds pork leg
- 1 Tablespoon butter
- 1 yellow onion, sliced
- garlic cloves, peeled and minced
- 2 Tablespoons ground cumin
- 2 Tablespoons ground thyme
- 2 Tablespoons ground chili
- 1 teaspoon salt
- 1 teaspoon fresh ground black pepper
- 1 cup hot water

Directions:

1 Butter the slow cooker. Slice crisscrosses along the top of the pork leg.
2 Arrange onion slices and minced garlic along the bottom of the slow cooker.
3 Place meat on top of vegetables.
4 In a small bowl, mix the herbs. Rub it all over the pork leg.
5 Add the water. Cover, cook on high for 8 hours.
6 Remove and transfer, cover with foil. Let it rest for 1 hour.
7 Shred the meat and serve.

Nutrition:
Calories: 143

Carbs: 0g
Fat: 3g
Protein: 28g

CPSIA information can be obtained
at www.ICGtesting.com
Printed in the USA
BVHW091502150221
600147BV00006B/530